Rational Simplicity

Rational Simplicity

Setting Course to a Simpler Life

Tim Covell

iUniverse, Inc.
New York Lincoln Shanghai

Rational Simplicity
Setting Course to a Simpler Life

Copyright © 2005 by Tim Covell

iUniverse books may be ordered through booksellers or by contacting:

iUniverse
2021 Pine Lake Road, Suite 100
Lincoln, NE 68512
www.iuniverse.com
1-800-Authors (1-800-288-4677)

ISBN: 0-595-34214-0

Printed in the United States of America

Table of Contents

PREFACE

This is a short book. I have not loaded it with examples. Many similar books are stuffed with text like, "Mary was a successful marketing executive, but her hectic life left her with little time for…." Some authors include anecdotes to get their manuscripts up to "book length." They use a lot of words, but say little. I have tried to do the opposite. You should be able to read this book in a few hours.

Similarly, this book is not a detailed road map for changing your life. It is an outline. The mechanics of simple living are easy. Everyone understands how to live simply, or could if they put their minds to it. The difficult thing about living simply is shifting your values and having the strength to swim against the stream of what most people do.

This book focuses on ideas and values. However, I do not assume that I know what is best for you. I do not set out nine mandatory steps to simple living. I do not expect you to agree with everything I say. In fact, you will likely disagree with some things I say. But please note, I am not saying that you *must* do anything described in this book. I am only asking you to consider the ideas. If you do not like what I say in one section, move to the next. Remember, there is no one path to simplicity.

I did not write this book with the goal of fame or fortune, but rather to share my experiences. The ideas in this book helped me. I hope they help you too.

INTRODUCTION

At age 42, I retired. I do not have a pension and I have never earned more than $25 an hour. I am not a millionaire. I have enough money to live comfortably. I do not use an alarm clock. I go to bed when I am tired. I wake when I am rested. I do not commute, dress up for work or worry about pleasing the boss.

Retirement has brought pleasant surprises. I have time to stop and talk with people. I can hold the door for the older person behind me—even if it means waiting an extra minute. I can drive the speed limit, go for walks, travel, read and research. I exercise regularly and live with little stress.

Along my path I have learned some things I wish to share with you.

I call the path "rational simplicity." It is a program with no rules. It has no steps, plans or excessive paperwork. It does, however, provide a series of suggestions that may help change your relationship with money.

At its core, simple living is living on less than you earn. But simple living also has the final goal of escaping from paid work and pursuing what is really important to you. The opposite of simple living is consumerism. Consumerism is the belief that things will make you happy. Simplicity is the acknowledgment that they will not.

Rational simplicity is not dictated by religion or philosophy, but rather by an analysis of choices. I believe that when you analyze the choices, isolated from the power of advertising, you will choose simplicity.

Rational simplicity also describes my approach. I do not believe you should eliminate purchases that bring you pleasure. I do not believe you should separate two ply toilet paper to save money. But I do believe simple changes can improve your life.

Getting ahead financially is similar to losing weight. The concepts behind weight loss are easy. You either exercise more, eat less, or both. Similarly, getting ahead financially is easy. You either spend less than you earn, invest, or both. Everyone can grasp these concepts. However, complex roadblocks keep us from achieving our goals. To diet successfully, you do not need to count calories as much as you need to change your relationship with food and exercise. Similarly, to get ahead financially it is not enough to budget. You need to change your values.

To help you change your values, I offer suggestions in the following chapters. Sticking with the diet theme, consider the chapters entrees. Just as you do not need to eat each entree at a restaurant, you need not consider each chapter a step. Sample the suggestions and use the ones that make sense. But before getting to the suggestions, I wish to give you examples of why change is necessary.

Life Out of Balance

Thoreau said, "the mass of men live lives of quiet desperation." I believe they do because they put their dreams on hold while they trade their days for unneeded consumer goods. This book encourages you to spend less time pursuing material goods and more time pursuing your dreams.

Symptoms abound that life for many Americans is out of balance. In the past 50 years, Americans have doubled their consumption of material goods; however, their level of happiness has not increased. The percentage of Americans reporting they are very happy peaked in 1957. Contrary to what advertisers would have you believe, consumer goods do not bring happiness. In fact, excessive consumption has put many on a work and spend treadmill that negatively affects health, happiness and family.

A look at things you experience every day provides additional evidence that life is out of balance.

Crazy Commuters

A sad indicator of how people choose to trade their time is how much they commute. The average worker commutes 49 minutes a day. Combined with working 45 hours a week (Americans now work more hours than most industrialized nations, surpassed only by Koreans and Czechs), that adds up to almost 50 hours a week away from important things, like family, friends and community.

Commuting, coupled with the stress of debt and lack of time, has led to a dangerous new breed of driver. I see them on a daily basis, usually driving a new car or sports utility vehicle, sometimes talking on a cell phone. I have plenty of time. I do not speed and I purposely choose routes with slower speed limits—often roads without passing lanes. These crazy commuters drive inches from my bumper. I look in the rear view mirror and see their faces contorted with rage that I dare to drive the speed limit. I always look for an opportunity to pull over and let them pass. They rush by at breakneck speed to their job, or to get their kids from school. I feel sorry for these people. And I feel sorry for the families they return to, full of pent up anger. The crazy commuters probably think that rushing is getting them ahead, but they are like hamsters on a treadmill, running like crazy but staying in place. By shifting values, they could get off the treadmill.

House Size

Huge houses are another sign that life is out of balance. Did you ever wonder why older houses are so much smaller? Why they have one or no garage? Why they only have one bathroom?

The average new house a generation ago had less than 1,000 square feet, a single bath and a one car garage. The average new house today is more than double that size, has two or more bathrooms and two or more garages. This is despite the fact that today's families are much smaller than those of the baby boom generation. Fifty years ago, only 20% of houses had more rooms than people living in them, today, the number has risen to 90%.

Another aspect of houses is closet size. Houses a century ago did not have closets. Clothes were stored in furniture. Houses 80 years ago had closets with about six square feet of floor space.

People 80 years ago were not so different from you and me. But they lived in an age when the advertising machine was not so sophisticated. They lived in a time when they worked less, owned less and were more satisfied. Today, many new homes have closets bigger than a bedroom. The owners work extra hours to buy extra space to store things they do not need. The excess consumer goods that make closets bulge have not brought happiness. Working extra hours to support huge houses and bulging closets shows that life is out of balance.

Cars

A better title to this section would be trucks, because more than 50% of new vehicles sold in America are trucks. Instead of buying fuel efficient automobiles, Americans are purchasing increasingly powerful gas hogs.

The Ford Excursion is a perfect example of excess. Too large to fit in a standard garage, the Excursion weighs 7,190 pounds (more than twice a Honda Accord), can be equipped with a ten-cylinder engine, which, combined with four wheel drive, costs $43,000 and takes you only 12 city miles on a gallon of gasoline. When financed, vehicles like the Excursion cost $900 a month for principal and interest, plus $100 for insurance. Someone living simply could make it on the monthly costs of the Excursion alone! Adding to the irony is that 80% of SUVs are never driven off-road. The great majority are used for commuting and ferrying children.

A generation ago, Volkswagen promoted the Beetle with the slogan, "small is beautiful." VW now makes a V-10 SUV and a

12-cylinder luxury car. No one needs a V-10 SUV, yet thousands of families a year are seduced into trading their time and money for this symbol of excess. The increasingly large, overpowered and high-priced vehicles clogging America's roads show that life is out of balance.

The Technological Circle

Not so long ago, futurists promised that labor saving devices would result in increased free time. New machines were supposed to create a leisure-based society. In fact, technologies like cell phones, email, computers and fax machines have resulted in work following us home. Instead of working less, the average American works 160 hours more than his counterpart of 20 years ago—an extra full month of work a year.

In fact, a generation ago, most families were supported by one breadwinner. In 1950, only 20% of families had two working parents. By 1990, that number tripled. Today, most families feel they need two working spouses. Advertisers have convinced us to trade more time to buy more goods, including the technology that was supposed to free us. Many families have a phone line, computer line, cable TV line, and one, two or three mobile phones. They have voice mail, call forwarding, call interrupting, caller ID, text messaging and more. It is not unusual for a family to spend $200 a month just to feel connected. When translated into time, if your real wage is $10 an hour (discussed in Chapter 3), you are working two and a half days a month just for the connections.

Technology has become a vicious circle. Cars cost more to incorporate features like power windows and satellite navigation. Satellite navigation on a new General Motors car initially costs over $2,000, plus between $17 and $70 a month. It makes no sense to trade five weeks of your life to have a satellite system that does what you could do with a $3 road map.

Technology was supposed to have set us free, but when we are convinced to work extra hours to get it, it has enslaved us. Working more to buy technology shows that life is out of balance.

Commercialization of Holidays

Another symptom of a system gone awry is the commercialization of holidays. A generation ago, the only holidays that involved significant spending were Christmas and Hanukkah. Halloween was celebrated with bobbing for apples and maybe carving a pumpkin, Easter with dying eggs. But there was no need to spend additional household dollars. Lately, I have been surprised to see people decorating their homes with Halloween lights—sort of like Christmas lights, but with orange jack o' lantern bulbs. Easter is celebrated with special flags and yard sil-houettes of rabbits and eggs. The liquor industry has made drinking holidays out of not only New Year's, but also St. Patrick's Day, Cinco de Mayo, Halloween, the Super Bowl and others. The advertising industry has convinced us that we need to spend additional dollars to enjoy holidays.

The grandest scandal of all is what has happened to Christmas and Hanukkah. The average family charges $1,150 during the holiday season. Some take a year or longer to recover from the holiday spending binge. The magic of a religious celebration has been perverted into a retail frenzy that leaves families stressed instead of happy. The commercialization of holidays shows that life is out of balance.

Rudeness

A recent study confirms that Americans are increasingly rude. But while bemoaning rudeness, the majority of people report that they have been rude to others. Perhaps goaded by stress, people are no longer willing to take time to say, "excuse me," hold the door for others, or participate in polite acts that make life a little kinder. Rudeness begets rudeness, increased stress, and in some instances, outpourings of rage. In the rush to get to work, commute home, and ferry the family to activities, we do not feel we have time to be polite to our neighbors. The increase in rudeness is a byproduct of elevating material things above people and shows that life is out of balance. A simpler lifestyle frees up time and engenders an attitude that allows a return to courtesy.

Children Raised by Televison

One of the saddest results of our consumer society is that fewer households elect to have a stay-at-home parent. When working parents are home, they are often preoccupied with neglected chores or seeking stress relief. Unfortunately, many families allow television to become a surrogate parent. American children interact with their parents 30 minutes a day, but spend 3.8 hours watching TV. They spend more time watching TV each year than they spend in school. TV, the most effective purveyor of advertising in the world, is teaching children how to live. When children spend more time with the TV than with their parents, life is out of balance.

Environmental Impact

The environmental impact of consumerism cannot be ignored. Most are aware that the United States has 5% of the world's population but consumes 25% of its natural resources and produces 25% of its waste.

On a personal level, look at the volume of trash you produce each week. Likely, your trash bin is bulging with the packaging and waste of what you consume. That alone may cause twinges of guilt, even without considering the energy consumed and toxic waste produced funding the consumer lifestyle. The disproportionate impact of the American lifestyle on the environment shows that life is out of balance.

Health Impact

Consumerism leads to a treadmill of working and spending. When you are worried about money, it is easy to put in a few extra hours at work. Work takes precedence, so you grab a burger for lunch, skip your evening exercise, and maybe settle down for a drink and some television before bed. An incredible 65% of Americans are overweight. Bad health costs billions in medical care, plus more importantly, causes pain and suffering for the individuals and their families. Unfortunately, the pursuit of consumer goods has left many with little time to attend to health.

Quiet Desperation

Everyone is going to die. But we live our lives in denial. Instead of thinking about how few precious days are left to achieve our goals, we set the alarm clock, cope with an unreasonable boss, swallow the stress of the day, return home, sleep and then do it again. So much time and talent are wasted pursuing material things that do not bring happiness.

People on the path to simplicity realize that consumer goods do not bring happiness. Instead, they shift from trading their time for consumer goods to focusing on what will bring happiness.

There is no single answer for what will bring happiness. Only you can define it. It could be raising a family, serving the church or community, playing an instrument masterfully, traveling overseas, climbing mountains or writing. There are as many definitions of happiness as there are people.

The suggestions in this book allow you to have more time to achieve your goals and find happiness. The suggestions in this book are simple, and here they are:

- Separate wants from needs;
- Think of money as time;
- Break the advertising chain;
- Avoid consumer debt;
- Know your net worth;
- Understand the magic of compound interest;
- Set goals;

◆   Choose a path to simplicity; and,

◆   Pursue your dream.

   Before you go to the suggestions, please complete the exercises in the next chapter.

CHAPTER 1

EXERCISES

Following are simple questions. Do not take a lot of time, write a simple answer. Jot down the first thing that comes to mind and move on. We will revisit these exercises later in the book, so you might want to put a paperclip or bookmark here.

1. Everyone maintains a mental list of their upcoming major purchases. Write a list of the next four major items you plan to buy (automobile, television, computer, digital camera, etc.).

2. Imagine that your house is on fire. All of the people are safe. You are able to return to the house to retrieve only three things. What are they?

3. I wish I had more _____.

4. I am sorry that I am too busy to _____.

5. If I had unlimited time, money and talent, I would _____ _____.

6. If I lost my job today I would _____.

7. My net worth is _____.

8. Write down the name of your favorite:
   Movie   _____
   Book   _____
   TV Show _____

9. The three most important things in the world to me are:

10.   The best time in my life was when_____.

CHAPTER 2

SEPARATE WANTS FROM NEEDS

What you *want* and what you *need* are different. Human needs are basic. Peter Menzel's book <u>Material World: A Global Family Portrait</u>, shows pictures of people around the world with all of their possessions in front of their homes (Figure 1). The book cover contrasts the abundant wealth of an American family with the simplicity of a family from Bhutan. Although each family holds religious artifacts as the items most valued, the contrast in lifestyles is startling. The great variance of material wealth demonstrates that desires are a product of culture and opportunity. The families from one country are no more happy than those from another.

Another researcher compared the happiness of people on the Forbes 400 list of richest people with the Maasai herdspeople of

East Africa. Despite the enormous disparity in monetary wealth, the two groups reported equal levels of happiness.

The photos of families around the world and the studies of happiness demonstrate both that humans do not need much and that material goods do not lead to happiness.

It is easy to desire things. A shiny new truck, a beautiful house, a date with a model, these are desires—things you do not need, yet may strive to get.

Needs are very basic. You need food, shelter and relationships. Hunter/Gatherer tribes spend only 15 hours a week fulfilling basic needs. Living in America, you likely could have these things without working at all, or if you did work, working only a few hours a week.

Some would argue that purchasing a house costs more than working full time at minimum wage can buy in many parts of the country. But by shelter, I am not talking about the American lifestyle. I am talking about someplace to keep you from succumbing to the elements. Homeless people likely find this type of shelter in a variety of ways in your city for no money whatsoever. The base line of what you need is very low.

Part of the cycle of consumerism is feeling that you *need* things. In fact, there is very little you actually need. Understanding that much of what you buy is a desire will help you to realize that you have choice.

In exercise one, you listed four anticipated major purchases. Go back to that list and note which are needs and which are desires. I am not suggesting that you forgo the purchases, only that you understand you are making a choice to purchase each. I also suggest that you evaluate that choice as described in the next chapter, by weighing how much of your time you are choosing to trade for the desired object.

Figure 1. Families with their material goods.
© Peter Menzel/www.menzelphoto.com.

CHAPTER 3

THINK OF MONEY AS TIME

Everyone is familiar with the phrase, "time is money." I agree. Money represents time, your precious time. By working, you trade your time for money. I suggest that you examine every purchase with this in mind.

I wish I were smart enough to have figured this out myself, but I learned it from a book called <u>Your Money or Your Life</u> by Joe Dominguez and Vicki Robin.

The most important lesson I see in their book is to calculate your real wage, then consider each purchase not in terms of dollars, but rather in terms of how much time you trade to make the purchase.

Your Real Wage

To calculate your real wage, start with your weekly take home pay, then subtract all the costs of your work. Consider the special clothing you wear, the transportation you use and the food you eat. Don't forget the drinks you may have to help forget about work and the vacation you take to get away from work.

Next, add up all the time you devote to work including preparing, commuting and decompressing. Don't forget any after-hours time you are obligated to spend with co-workers and any studying you do to help you get ahead at work.

Finally, divide your pay, minus all the incidental expenses, by the number of hours a week you devote to work. The resulting figure is your real wage.

For example:

Weekly:

Hours at work	48 hours
Preparation time	4 hours
Commute time	5 hours
Recovery time	3 hours
Total hours devoted to work	60 hours

Salary:

Weekly take home pay	$740
Food cost	- $35
Commute cost	- $50
Liquor cost	- $25
Specialized clothing cost	- $30
Total money from work	$600

Six hundred dollars income, divided by 60 hours devoted to work, equals $10.00 an hour real wage ($600 ÷ 60 = $10). In effect, the person in this example trades one hour of his time for $10.

Now, here is the genius in Dominguez and Robin's book. Divide the cost of every purchase by your real wage and consider how much time you are trading. For example, if a new CD costs $15.00, divide the cost by $10 and ask if you are willing to give up one and a half hours of your life to own the CD. Maybe you desire a new microwave oven. Is a $150 microwave worth 15 hours of your life? How about a new car? Is a Hyundai worth half a year? Is a Honda worth a year of your life?

After learning this formula I stopped driving a new car. Like many people, I thought I needed a new car. I drove a lot for work and eventually my old car left me stranded in a rural area. I financed a new Honda Accord. After driving the Honda for a few months, the novelty wore off. One day, while I was making my hour commute to work, I figured out that just owning the new car with full coverage insurance cost 25% of my take home pay—before I even pulled out of the driveway. I asked myself if I was willing to trade one week a month to have the new car. My answer was no. Luckily, I was able to sell the car for almost as much as I paid for it. I bought a reliable used car for cash and proceeded to apply the lesson to other parts of my life.

Understanding this concept changed my relationship with money and started me on the path to simplicity. Each and every purchase should be considered something you trade your life for. If you conclude the purchase is worth it, proceed. But likely you will find many things are much less desirable when viewed this way.

That's it. If you take nothing else from this book, do this: calculate your real wage and consider each purchase as spending your precious time.

Return to the list of anticipated purchases you made in exercise one. Calculate how many hours of your life you will trade for the purchase. Does the planned purchase seem worth the time, or would you rather spend your time doing something else? Would the money be better spent on investments to free you from work?

As you begin using this formula, I believe you will spend less of your time (and money) on consumer goods and will focus more on what is really meaningful to you.

CHAPTER 4

BREAK THE ADVERTISING CHAIN

Advertisers do not want you to focus on the difference between wants and needs. They want you to think you need what you desire. For example, cars are not needs. You can get to work by bike or public transit. If you live in a place where neither is practical, you can move closer to work. A car is a desire.

Advertisers sell discontent. They want you to think that what you have is not good enough. When you were a teenager and desired a car, you probably would have settled for anything that ran. Since then, you have likely been convinced to trade up to newer and fancier models. When you have a Hyundai, you likely desire a Honda. From a Honda you wish to move to a BMW, and so on.

Automakers developed the model year change to create discontent—to convince people that their old car was no longer good enough and only a new model would do. Advertisers try to convince you that you need their product to be happy, but as soon as you buy it, they say it is not good enough and you need a better one.

By playing on basic human motivations, advertisers convince you that you need more and more—even to the degree that you are irrational. It is irrational to spend so much time at work that you neglect your family—but many people do. We call them workaholics. It is irrational to allow debt and stress to break families apart, but the most frequent reason for divorce is disagreement over money.

Advertisers have no stake in your happiness, they have a single goal, convincing you to buy more. They do not care how many hours you work to buy their product. They do not care about the impact working those hours has on your family. They do not care that your desire for a car, boat, or suburban mansion causes you to neglect the things you need. All they care about is that you buy their product.

Advertisers are good at what they do. They even create desire where there is no basis in need. Advertisers have made a combination of sugar water and caffeine one of the most valuable brand names in the world—Coca Cola. But at least with Coke you get *something* for your money. A better example of the power of advertising is bottled water. An unbiased study demonstrated that the healthiest and best tasting water is New York City tap water. However, countless consumers unnecessarily pay between one and two dollars for ten ounces of water they could get for free at a water fountain.

Another example of the power of advertising is found in sports utility vehicles. An expensive and fuel consuming option on many vehicles is four wheel drive. Eighty percent of sports utility vehicles are never driven off the road, yet the great majority are equipped with four wheel drive. If the primary purpose of four wheel drive were not to impress others, it would be an unannounced feature of the vehicle; instead, it is touted four or five times on the vehicle and on some it is advertised in six inch tall letters bragging "4 x 4." For most, four wheel drive is not used for climbing mountains, it is used to say, "I am the kind of sporty, rugged person who *could* climb mountains." Just like the desire for bottled water, for most the desire for four wheel drive is created by advertising.

Advertising also shapes values. It takes natural inclinations and steers them toward purchasing. For example, a young woman may be interested in meeting a man who will be a good parent. Advertising takes this inclination and manipulates it. Chevrolet tries to convince her that an attractive man is a man who drives a Corvette convertible. At the same time, Chevrolet works to convince men that young women are attracted to

Corvette drivers. Many people buy the advertising line and think that men who drive Corvette convertibles are successful and perhaps "sexy."

But you can break the advertising chain by thinking for yourself. The Corvette is an expensive gas hog. It burns premium gas, sells for $50,000 and if financed costs $1,000 per month. An alternate opinion of a man who drives a Corvette is that he is an irresponsible spendthrift who does not care about the environment. Further, if you are thinking about a long term relationship, the blond in the convertible is a lot more likely to get skin cancer and may not be around long enough to be a good parent to your children.

Flashy cars impress, but more than half of all new luxury cars are leased. The drivers do not even buy them, they rent the ability to impress. In fact, Thomas Stanley and William Danko, in The Millionaire Next Door, empirically demonstrated that the car most likely to be driven by a millionaire is not a Jaguar, BMW or Mercedes, but rather a four-door American car like the police drive—a Crown Victoria or Impala. Advertising creates a false link between luxury cars and success. In fact, real millionaires drive boring, reliable cars. By breaking the advertising chain you can free yourself of the pressure to buy things to feel successful. A truer feeling of success is knowing you are financially secure enough to not work, rather than driving a flashy car but knowing you would lose it if you missed two paychecks.

My path to simplicity has come not only from living conservatively, but from investing in real estate. I discuss this more in the Epilogue. I made a similar shift in values involving cars and the ability to buy real estate. In my early days looking at houses, I thought my modest car would give the impression that I could not afford to buy. I used to think an expensive car meant that people could afford an expensive house. But I was wrong. As I became more involved in selling houses, I learned that many people cannot afford to buy because they are saddled with a high car payment. Additionally, many are "upside down" in their loans because they owe more than the used car would bring if sold. Time after time I have found that people with flashy cars are not good home buyers.

Twice, I have sold homes to people who paid cash. The first time was to a couple who drove a faded, dented, 15-year-old Toyota mini-pickup. The second time was to a single woman driving an older Dodge minivan. Now, when I see someone with a modest car, I am more impressed. I perceive that the person knows how to manage money and is much more likely to be able to purchase the house. Experience has taught me to break the advertising chain which links expensive cars with success.

Another reinforcement for breaking the link between expensive cars and success is to look at the cars in apartment parking lots. You will see many new, expensive cars. Although these apartment dwellers appear successful while driving, many do not have the ability to buy a house. Think of it, would you rather have a nice house (which will likely appreciate in value); or share your walls with other apartment dwellers, but look successful when driving down main street in your quickly depreciating car?

Advertisers spend billions of dollars a year refining and communicating their message. Advertising creeps into our lives through the TV we watch, the radio we hear and the magazines we read. There is little to counter it. Even the President of the United States said it is our patriotic duty to shop. There are a thousand glitzy ads saying a great way to relax is to visit Club Med, Las Vegas or Disneyland. There are few voices encouraging you to take your vacation hiking in a national park. There are millions of messages asking you to spend. Only a few religious practitioners and independent thinkers encourage you to conserve. The masses follow the easy path, work and spend. The masses lead lives of quiet desperation. But you can think for yourself and break the cycle. You have the opportunity to separate needs from wants and to free your time to pursue the things that are really important.

In exercise ten, you recalled the best time in your life. Think back to that time. Where did you live, what did you drive and how much money was in your wallet? Many people recall the early days of their marriage, a low-budget trip, or a time in school. For most, the best times had little to do with material wealth. Expensive products rarely have a role in your fondest memories. Think of this the next time advertisers try to link expensive products with happiness.

In exercise two, you made a list of three things you would retrieve if your house were burning. Take a look at that list now. Likely the list did not contain the most expensive things in your house, but rather things with sentimental value like photos, heirlooms, or precious letters. Likely the three things center on relationships. But when you look at how you use your days, you probably devote far more time to earning money for consumer goods than you spend with your loved ones. It would be laughable to suggest that you trade your child, parent, spouse or best friend for consumer goods, but when you look at how you use your time, it may appear you are doing just that. Perhaps these relationships should receive more attention than the consumer goods that fill your home. By breaking the advertising chain you can stop elevating consumer goods over the things that are really important.

Breaking the chain between advertising and your values is difficult. The multibillion dollar industry uses complex psychological tools to influence you. It takes a strong will to buck the crowds and think for yourself. However, certain strategies can help.

Think for Yourself

First, think for yourself. As discussed earlier in this chapter, you can realize that fancy cars do not show success and that a bike rider makes a better date than a Corvette driver. Apply the same kind of analysis to other advertising influenced assumptions. The more you recognize the falseness of advertising, the easier it is to transfer the lesson to new situations.

Practice Avoidance

The second strategy is avoidance. An excellent example is the Sunday paper. If you are like most consumers, you look forward to reading the glossy advertising inserts. Rarely do you go to the ads because you are shopping for a particular item. You go to be seduced. You look at the ads to be convinced you need something they are selling, or that you can save money on something you did not know you wanted. Often ads lure you into the store where you purchase one or more items that you did not even think about before opening the Sunday paper. Stay away from ads, unless you are looking to buy something that you have decided is worth trading your time for. Only then should you begin shopping for the best deal.

Following in the same vein, many people shop for recreation. Some even shop for comfort. Terms like "retail therapy" and "shopaholic" are a sad commentary on how people seek solace in material things. My suggestion is that you do not enter a store (or heaven forbid, a mall) without deciding in advance what you want to buy. When you are tempted to buy something unplanned, put it down and think about it. Is it a need or a want? Is it worth trading your precious time for? Would the money be put to better use trying to reach your real goals?

Eliminate TV

The third strategy, eliminating TV, is another form of avoidance, but merits separate attention. Eliminating TV sounds radical, but the most effective purveyor of advertising is television. Elizabeth Shur, in her book <u>The Overspent American</u>, theorizes that TV encourages more spending because we no longer compare ourselves with our neighbors, but compare ourselves with our "friends" on TV. Besides being clever and good looking, TV characters live lifestyles far beyond the means of real people. Look at any popular show. The homes, furniture, automobiles, dinners and vacations of working class characters would break the budgets of real people making twice as much. Ms. Shur says that we compare ourselves with them and feel we should be able to maintain a similar lifestyle. Our inability to live like our friends on TV encourages us to borrow to try to be like them. Ms. Shur supported her hypothesis with research that found people who watched the most TV reported the lowest levels of savings and the highest levels of unhappiness.

In exercise eight, you wrote the name of your favorite book, movie and TV show. You likely read the book and saw the movie more than a year ago, but you still remember the plot and the message it carried. I challenge you to tell me the plot of your favorite TV show that aired this week a year ago. I bet you cannot. Like cotton candy, TV provides little substance. It wastes time and encourages you to consume more.

In exercise three, when asked the question, "I wish I had more…," most people respond, "time." TV eats up 3 hours and 42 minutes of the average American's day. By age 65, that's nine years of TV! Find some time, turn off the TV. Better yet, dispose of it entirely. TV is not harmless static. It is the most effective advertising medium known to man. Without TV, you will significantly reduce the effect of advertising and increase your happiness.

Substitute Solutions

The fourth strategy to break the advertising chain is to substitute solutions. Consider the goal you are trying to accomplish with a purchase and see if there is another way to achieve it. For example, when I was younger and dated, I realized that a good haircut can get you a date as easily as a Corvette. At that time, a good haircut cost $20 while a Corvette cost $20,000. Although a $20 haircut sounds extravagant, it saved me money because I used it as a substitute for buying an expensive car.

The point behind this is that you may be able to accomplish the same end for less. When you find yourself longing for a new car because you want your friends or co-workers to think well of you, search for another way to do it. Would volunteering for the neighborhood association earn your neighbors' respect? Would bicycling to work and losing 20 pounds impress the person you want to date more than a new car? By identifying the values you seek to fulfill with a purchase, you can sometimes fulfill the same desire for much less money.

Use a Carrot

The final strategy is using a carrot. An old story is that if you dangle a carrot from a stick in front of a horse, it will keep walking in hopes of reaching the carrot. Similarly, you have a dream to pursue. Escaping from work will allow you more time to pursue it. The dream is your carrot. Understanding, for example, that forgoing a new car now will allow you to travel the world later can help you counter the power of advertising.

Advertising permeates our lives. It is one of the most powerful forces in our society. But by realizing advertisers have no stake in your happiness, you can begin to break the advertising chain. You can lessen your exposure, for example, by turning off the TV, skipping the Sunday newspaper ads and staying out of the malls. And when you encounter advertising, you can think for yourself and work to rationally disconnect the advertiser's desired link between consumer goods and happiness. You can try to substitute solutions to attain the goal suggested by the advertiser by other means, and you can use your dream as a carrot to help you to ignore the advertising. Remember, consumer goods will not make you happy, but freeing up time to pursue your goals will.

CHAPTER 5

AVOID CONSUMER DEBT

The average American family spends 18% of its annual income on consumer debt. Consumer debt includes cars and credit cards but does not include mortgages. The average credit card debt is $9,000. If you make minimum payments on a card with 18% interest, it will take 31 years to pay off.

Everything purchased on credit effectively costs more. Consumer debt means trading your tomorrows to live well today. It is the opposite of investing. Consumer credit is a partner in crime with advertising. Together they encourage spending money you do not have on things you do not need. A byproduct of consumer debt is stress and family conflict. Most people are bound to jobs they do not like because they have little or no savings and a pile of debt. Many families are one or two paychecks away from disaster. Consumer debt should be avoided.

Charge cards are a recent invention. American Express, a charge card pioneer, began in 1949. Visa (then BankAmericard) started in 1958, MasterCard in 1966, and Discover in 1985. The advent of consumer credit coincides with the birth of television and the explosion of consumerism. Since then, people spend more, have more, but are no more happy.

The consumer credit industry is evolving. For example, when I was in college, it was difficult to get a credit card. The industry wanted students to graduate, earn money and pay bills responsibly before extending credit. Perhaps they were accidentally encouraging good spending habits. But they have learned. Now credit is extended freely to college students who start spending their tomorrows while still in school. Fifty-two percent of college freshmen carry credit cards. By the time they are sophomores, that number increases to 92%. Students double their average credit card debt and triple the number of credit cards in their wallets from the time they start college until graduation. The average college student has a $2,327 credit card balance that takes almost 20 years to pay off with minimum payments. The credit industry has learned to seduce youths into a cycle of spending and borrowing.

Consumer lenders are increasingly sophisticated in convincing Americans that trading their tomorrows to live well today is acceptable. But the consumer debt they sell keeps many on a work and spend treadmill that does not allow time for the really important things in life.

If the average American family could delay gratification long enough to pay off their consumer debt and not incur any more, they could have 18% more money. Invested, that money compounded over time would produce enough income to allow them to pursue their dreams. Eighteen percent of the average family income of $62,000 is $925 per month. That sum, invested over 20 years at 10%, would create a nest egg of over $700,000. Over 30 years, it would amount to more than $2 million. Simply investing the amount the average family pays to service debt can provide the freedom to focus on the truly important things in life.

Mortgage Debt Distinguished

Consumer debt involves financing quickly depreciating assets. For example, a new Dodge Neon ES costs $14,000. When financed over five years at 9%, the loan balance after two years is $9,300, while the market value is only $6,000. This is known as being "upside down" in the loan. If you sold the car for $6,000, you would have to reach in your pocket for $3,300 more to pay off the loan and break even.

But not all debt is bad. Some debt can be used to make money. The most common example is mortgage debt. For most, homes are a leveraged investment. The typical owner buys a home with 20%, 10%, or even 3% down. That leverage, combined with even modest increases in home values, can make mortgage debt a good investment. For example, if you purchase a $100,000 home with $10,000 down and real estate prices increase only 1% next year, you still get a 10% return on your money. However, if real estate accelerates 10% in value, you gain 100% ($10,000 gain on a $10,000 investment). If ten years ago you put $10,000 down on a $100,000 home that appreciated 6% per year, your home would now be worth $160,000, a sixfold increase and an annualized return of 60%. Sometimes debt can be good, but only where the returns justify the risk.

CHAPTER 6

KNOW YOUR NET WORTH

Exercise seven asked, "What is your net worth?" If you were unable to answer that question, you are like a dieter who is unwilling to step on the scale. Perhaps you think that by not looking you can avoid facing reality. But to make progress toward your financial goals, you should know where you are now.

Just like everyone knows how to lose weight, everyone knows how to calculate net worth. You add up all of your debt and compare it to the value of everything you own.

When you apply for a mortgage, the bank makes you calculate your net worth on the mortgage application. If you recently applied for a mortgage, you can pull out the application and update it. But on your personal calculation, be sure to use realistic values. Do not put down the cost of your furniture and electronics, but rather what you could get for them if you had a yard sale. Do not put down the retail value of your car unless you are confident you could sell it for that price. Keep your personal net worth statement accurate. It will help you measure your financial progress.

If you already track your net worth, skip to the next subsection. Otherwise, take the time right now to pencil in your best guess on the following chart. Later, pull out the bills and the mortgage statement and put in exact figures. If you don't start now, you may continue your avoidance behavior and never do the calculation.

Assets:	Total Value	Monthly Income
Bank Accounts	$	$
Money Market Accounts	$	$
Certificates of Deposit	$	$
Savings Bonds	$	$
Stocks	$	$
Bonds	$	$
Mutual Funds	$	$
Government Securities	$	$
Employee Stock Options	$	$
Investment Real Estate	$	$
Cash Value of Life Insurance	$	$
Surrender Value of Annuities	$	$

Pension	$	$
IRA/KEOGH	$	$
Home	$	$
Vacation Real Estate	$	$
Tools and Equipment	$	$
Furniture and Electronics	$	$
Automobiles	$	$
Recreational Vehicles	$	$
Jewelry and Collectibles	$	$
Precious Metals and Coins	$	$
Value of Business	$	$
Loans Payable to You (Real Estate Contracts, Deeds of Trust, Loans to Children)	$	$
Other	$	$
Other	$	$
Other	$	$
Total Assets	$	$

Debts: Total Liability   Monthly Pmt.

Home Mortgage	$	$
Home Equity Line of Credit	$	$
Other Mortgages or Notes	$	$
Student Loans	$	$
Vehicle Loans	$	$

Taxes Due	$	$
Credit Card 1	$	$
Credit Card 2	$	$
Credit Card 3	$	$
Credit Card 4	$	$
Other	$	$
Other	$	$
Other	$	$
Total Debt	$	$
Plus Total Assets (from previous section)	$	$
Equals Net Worth	$	$

I picture net worth as a cross-section of the earth. Most of the earth is covered by water and the ocean has underwater valleys. Being deep in debt is like being in an underwater valley. Someone with zero net worth is at sea level. Many people live somewhere on the land or mountains (having a positive net worth) and some live up in the clouds—where their money frees them to skip work and focus on what is really important. Find where your net worth falls on the following diagram (Figure 2). Here are a few comments about each status.

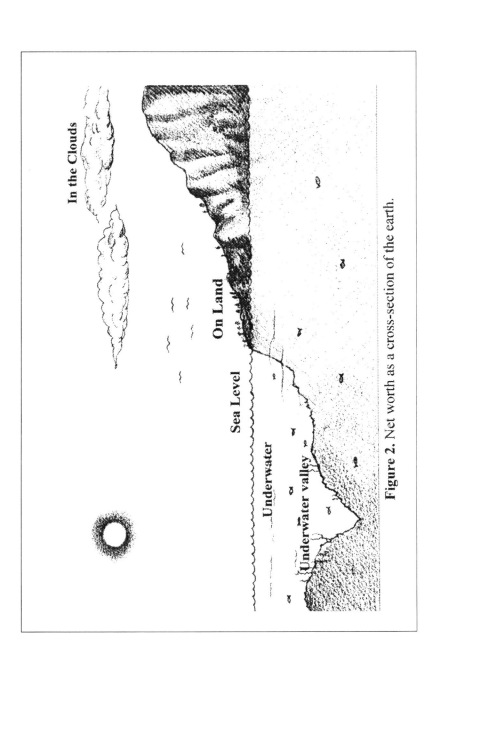

Figure 2. Net worth as a cross-section of the earth.

Underwater Valley

People whose debts far exceed their assets are a long way from being free of the work and spend cycle. If you are in this category, calculate the maximum amount you can pay on your consumer debt (not including mortgages) per month. If it would take more than two years to pay all the bills, talk to a bankruptcy attorney.

Whether bankruptcy is a good option depends on your income, debts, assets and personal values. An attorney should provide a free consultation and give expert advice on the pros and cons for your particular situation.

Despite its stigma, bankruptcy is a legitimate tool to gain a fresh start. Bankruptcy can eliminate all consumer debt and bring you up to "sea level" in a matter of months. The danger is using bankruptcy and then returning to old habits. However, if you make the values changes suggested in this book, bankruptcy may be the quickest step up to a simpler life style.

An alternative to bankruptcy is offered by Consumer Credit Counseling. The credit industry funds this nonprofit organization with the goal of keeping you paying your bills. When faced with the alternative of getting nothing from a bankrupt borrower, most creditors will waive interest and late fees and allow the borrower to pay back the loan more quickly. Consumer Credit Counseling sometimes neglects to tell you that bankruptcy may be a better option. But if bankruptcy is unavailable, or if you are morally opposed to bankruptcy, Consumer Credit Counseling is an alternative.

A short cut like bankruptcy, or diligent payment, can bring you up from the depths of debt.

Underwater

For those whose debts are manageable, but who have negative net worth, the path to simplicity begins by not incurring more consumer debt. But this is not enough. Making minimum payments on a $9,000 credit card balance at 18% interest takes 31 years to pay off. For real progress, you need an accelerated repayment schedule. A number of websites help you see how long it will take to get out of debt, for example, cgi.money.cnn.com/tools/debtplanner/debtplanner.jsp. The theory behind all plans is the same. Begin paying as much as possible on your highest interest consumer debt. Make minimum payments on the remaining debts. When you have paid off the first debt, begin maximum payments on the next highest interest debt, and so forth, until all of the debts are paid.

In paying debts, it helps to make a wall chart or to track it on a computer. Then you can make it a game. When you get a tax refund, put it toward debt reduction and chart it. Do the same with your year-end bonus. If you skip dinner out, put the cost toward debt reduction. If you need more help, dozens of library books and websites describe how to get out of debt. The technique is not difficult, but the choice to do so is. However, when you rationally consider the alternatives, getting out of debt is the best course to a simpler lifestyle. When you shift to valuing debt reduction over material acquisition, you will make surprisingly quick progress.

On Land

About a half of all Americans have a positive net worth. But for most, their home is the asset that brings them into positive territory. Further, their work and spend lifestyle gives them little hope of getting off the treadmill.

The challenge for people with a positive net worth who pursue simplicity is to examine their spending and savings to optimize progress to the goal of not working for money.

For example, someone with a $300,000 net worth might seem pretty lucky. But if that sum is equity in a primary residence, it may be unproductive. By selling the home and carrying back a real estate contract for $150,000 (at 8% over 30 years), then buying a simpler home for $150,000, the homeowner could create a

$1,100 per month stream of income—perhaps enough to set him free to pursue his dreams.

Take a look back at the assets on your net worth chart. Are any unproductive? Are some under productive? Maybe you have $5,000 in an interest-free checking account that you could move into an interest-bearing FDIC insured money market account. Maybe a savings account at a local bank is earning half of what it could at one of the top paying banks listed on Bankrate.com. Change is easier when you realize you are progressing more quickly toward your goal of not working for money.

A family with $50,000 in savings that currently spends every dollar it earns faces a different challenge. They need to evaluate their spending more carefully and shift some of it to savings. Applying the values described in this book will help. A tool to detect where savings are possible is to write down everything you spend for a month, then look at the list for potential savings.

For example, even though I live relatively frugally, I recently reexamined my spending. To start, an Internet service I initially got for free with a computer had become a $23 a month charge card debit. I switched to a less expensive provider for $10 a month. I also was able to save $7 a month on my gym membership by shifting to daytime only use. Similarly, a cell phone I once had for business outlived its usefulness. I canceled the service, saving $35 a month, but also had the choice of moving to a "pay as you go" service for $5 a month. Although the $55 monthly savings does not sound like much, invested at 10% over 40 years (as described in Chapter 7), it will grow to $347,824.

In the Clouds

Living in the clouds is the opposite of drowning in consumer debt. It is a status where investments provide enough money to live comfortably without working. Although you can enjoy a simple lifestyle without living in the clouds, you will find the greatest benefits when work is no longer necessary and you may devote as much time as you desire to the activities that are most important to you.

At this point, I wish to caution about what I call the money magazine factor. I recall a friend of mine emphatically telling me he needed $2 million to retire. The more I disagreed with him, the more strident he became. He felt he needed that much because an article in a popular magazine said so. Although his lifestyle was not too different from mine, his beliefs shackled him to scores of years of work because of what the "experts" said.

Money magazines say you need several million dollars to retire. But as you page through the magazines, look at the advertisers. They are overwhelmingly mutual funds and stock brokers whose survival depends on your business. The advertisers want you to keep working and investing with them as long as possible. Money magazines disregard the possibility of simple living.

In contrast, Joe Dominguez, who co-wrote Your Money or Your Life, stopped working when he had $100,000 and never worked for money again. Obviously, my friend who feels he needs $2 million will pay a lot more to money magazine advertisers than Joe Dominguez. Another interesting fact is that Joe Dominguez quit working when he was 31. He died when he was 56. Because he chose simplicity he had 25 years living as he pleased without the need for paid work. If he had followed the standard course of retiring at 62, he would have died before he had a chance to pursue his dreams.

To live in the clouds requires an income producing nest egg. I use the terms "nest egg" and "net worth" differently. "Net worth" is the value of everything you own. "Nest egg" is money that produces income. For example, if your sole possession is a pleasure boat worth $100,000, you have a net worth of $100,000, but no nest egg. If you sell the boat and invest the $100,000 in rental real estate, you will have shifted the money to your nest egg.

On the path to simplicity, you will find yourself spending less and less. When you acknowledge that things will not make you happy, each month you will have money to spare. After a while, your monthly expenses will stabilize. And whether the sum is $500 per month or $3,000, you can calculate the nest egg necessary to support life in the clouds with this formula:

monthly living expenses x 12 ÷ rate of return = nest egg

For example, someone who lives very simply may desire $500 per month. If he is able to earn 10% on his money, he will find he requires a $60,000 nest egg with this calculation:

$500 per month x 12 ÷ 10% = $60,000.

Another family may desire $3,000 a month. At the same rate of return, their formula looks like this:

$3,000 per month x 12 ÷ 10% = $360,000.

Simple living shrinks the size of the nest egg required to free you from paid work. Combining simple living and investing allows you to escape paid work far earlier than most.

CHAPTER 7

UNDERSTAND THE MAGIC OF COMPOUND INTEREST

There is an old saying that it takes money to make money. It is true. But you do not need a large sum of money to get started because of the magic of compound interest. You probably remember building a snowman as a child. You started with a fist size ball of snow and rolled it on the ground. Pretty soon it got too big for you and all of your friends to roll. The larger it became, the faster it grew.

The same thing happens to money. For example, if you save $100 a month for 40 years with no interest, you will put away $48,000. But if you invest that money at 10% interest, at the end of 40 years you have $632,407 (Figure 3). The interest earns interest and snowballs into a sizeable sum. It is like a charge card in reverse. Instead of something costing more because you finance it, your money earns more because you invest it.

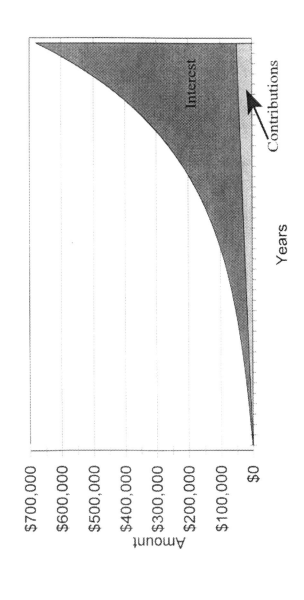

Figure 3. Over time, the interest earned on an investment far exceeds the amount contributed.

The magic of compound interest makes small savings more meaningful. For example, if you are a smoker who quits smoking, you will save $28 a week. If you invest that sum at 10% interest, in ten years you will have $22,942, in twenty, $85,049 and in forty, $708,296. By viewing the result through the lens of compound interest, suddenly small weekly savings become important.

Another example of small savings adding up is the cost of eating lunch out. If you bring a sack lunch and save $7.50 a day, five days a week, invested at 10%, in 20 years you will have $107,390, and over a typical 40 year career you will have saved $829,861. It makes sitting at your desk with a sack lunch seem wise instead of silly.

Comparing two automobiles and applying the magic of compound interest also shows where savings are found. The Dodge Durango 4WD has about the same cargo capacity as the Volkswagen Jetta Wagon. But the Dodge has a combined EPA rating of 15 miles per gallon, while the Jetta Diesel gets 41 miles per gallon. According to government statistics, each year the Dodge will cost $2,031 in gas for a typical driver, while the Jetta will burn only $809 of fuel. That $1,222 dollar a year difference, invested at 10%, will add up to $77,326 in 20 years, and $4,796,466 over a typical 60 year driving career. Small choices can make a big difference.

Almost every family could squeeze an extra $50 or $100 out of their monthly budget. But because they do not understand the magic of compound interest, they don't even try. They think that skipping mocha lattes, disconnecting cable and canceling the cell phone is too much of a sacrifice. But by shifting values, they could use these small savings to fund their retirement.

You can find information about how to save money in books at the library or online at sites like www.ftc.gov/bcp/conline/pubs/general/66ways.htm. You can calculate the impact of small savings using a computer program like Quicken or Microsoft Money, or at online sites such as www.hughchou.org/calc/.

The magic of compound interest is an essential tool for escaping from paid work. By living on less than you earn and investing the savings, you can make it to the clouds—where your nest egg earns enough to set you free from paid work.

Rates of Return

While discussing compound interest, I wish to comment on rates of return. Most people dream of finding a great investment that will accelerate them toward retirement. Investing in the stock market over the past 50 years has returned an average 10% per year. I use that figure frequently in this book. Looking at more recent figures, the Vanguard Index 500 fund returned an annualized 10.93% over the past ten years and 12.17% since it started in 1976. So, although the 10% figure I use may seem high, readily available investments can produce even higher rates of return.

Another passive investment with a decent rate of return is the real estate contract. Sometimes when you sell a house you act like a bank and lend the buyer money. Performance on the loan is secured by the house. If the buyer does not pay, you take the house back. Depending on where you live, this arrangement may be called a real estate contract or deed of trust. Currently, first position real estate contracts on properties you know can earn a relatively safe 8% rate of return. Most of my nest egg is in real estate contracts.

Real estate contracts are also bought and sold as a separate commodity (without previously owning the underlying real property), often at a discount to face value. For example, an $80,000 real estate contract at 8% interest might be sold to an investor for $70,000 cash. Buying real estate contracts at a discount can significantly increase the rate of return. To learn more about real estate contracts, ask an experienced investor or real estate attorney in your area.

Understanding the magic of compound interest and finding investments with a good rate of return will move you more quickly along your path to simplicity.

CHAPTER 8

SET GOALS

When goals are mentioned, many people think of budgets. Budgets are a lot like writing down everything you eat to help on a diet, it works for some people. If you are one of these people, I encourage you to make a budget and to stick with it.

I do not keep a budget. I have found that the strategies described in this book allow me to achieve the same ends without added paperwork. I try to separate my wants from my needs. I evaluate my wants in terms of how many hours of my life I am trading to acquire an object and I have no consumer debt. I do not watch TV and I strive to break the advertising chain. I use compound interest to make my savings grow. Another strategy that helps me considerably is setting financial goals.

Setting financial goals has had a magical effect on my life. When I first set financial goals, I was unsure I could achieve them. For example, the first goal I set was to get out of debt in a short period of time. After that, I sought to increase my net worth in annual increments, sometimes by as much as $100,000. Amazingly, once I set the goal, I almost invariably achieved it.

Goals can be useful on a daily, monthly, annual and long term basis. Consider, at a minimum, setting a long term financial goal that will put you in the clouds, for example, building a nest egg of $300,000. Additionally, consider breaking the steps to that goal into annual increments. For example, you might want to eliminate all charge card debt the first year and build up a $10,000 nest egg the second year. Establishing a $300,000 nest egg would take about 13 more years saving at the same pace.

Sometimes people complain that waiting 15 years for retirement is too long. They say, "in 15 years I'll be 45!" I reply, "how old you will be in 15 years if you don't save?" Of course, the answer is, "the same age." The future will come, whether you plan for it or not. Wouldn't you rather be 45 and free of work, than 45 and doing the same thing you are doing today?

The best explanation for why setting goals works is that once you set goals you align your values to achieve them. Lots of books and websites provide suggestions for reducing expenses and increasing savings. Setting goals starts you searching for these savings and moves you along the path to simplicity.

I do not wish to belabor the point, but rather to get you to try the strategy. Do you remember the chart of net worth as a cross section of the earth? Take a look at where you fall on the diagram. Then, using the formula at the end of Chapter 6, estimate the nest egg it will take for you to live in the clouds. Write it on the chart. Next, set a high but achievable goal of where you would like to be next year. Write it on the chart (See example in Figure 4). Finally, mark your calendar to revisit that page a year from now. You will be amazed that once you set the goal, you will shift your values to achieve or exceed it.

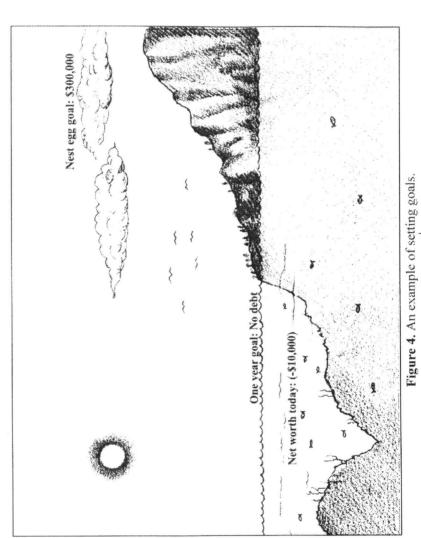

Nest egg goal: $300,000

One year goal: No debt

Net worth today: (-$10,000)

Figure 4. An example of setting goals.

CHAPTER 9

CHOOSE A PATH TO SIMPLICITY

The paths to simplicity are as varied as the people on them. There is no single way to a simple lifestyle. The previous chapters suggest ways to shift your values. Following are examples of how reducing expenses and investing can free you from work.

The 10% Solution

A classic recommendation is to invest 10% of your income. If you start early enough, over time the savings will compound to the point you no longer need to work.

For example, if a 20-year-old worker earns $20,000 a year and saves 10% of his salary ($167 a month) at 10% interest, at age 44 he will have a nest egg large enough to allow him to stop working and collect $22,000 a year. There are many books on investing at the library or bookstore which discuss the 10% solution in detail.

The 18% Solution (No Consumer Debt)

Many families have a hard time imagining where they could find 10% of their income to save, no less 18%. But as discussed in Chapter 5, the average American family could save 18% of their income per year *without* significantly altering their lifestyle if they could eliminate consumer debt and shift that money to savings. In just 19 years, the savings would produce enough income to allow them to stop working.

No New Car

Payments on an average new car with full coverage insurance eat up $600 or more per month. Perfectly reliable transportation cars can be purchased for a fraction of the cost of new. When I commuted 130 miles a day and drove around the state for my job, I put many miles on my car. By shopping carefully, I could buy a reliable used car from the original owner with 50,000 miles, put another 49,000 miles on the car and sell it with just under 100,000 miles for the price I paid in the first place. I was able to use a perfectly reliable car for almost no cost. Families who regularly purchase one or more new cars could otherwise live exactly as they do today but accrue significant savings by driving used cars.

Imagine, simply by giving up driving a new car and investing the $600 payment, you could quit working and retire with over a million dollars in just 28 years. If you put $600 a month away at 10% interest over the typical 60 year driving career, you would have more than $28 million.

The Housing Two-Step

Federal tax law allows homeowners to sell their primary residence and pocket the gain tax-free every two years. The tax law provides a great way to build wealth—although it requires frequent moves.

I have taken advantage of the tax law and sold my home every two years. Although moving frequently sounds difficult, it can be fun. Moving encourages you to reduce the quantity of consumer goods you own. It also decreases your desire to buy more—anything you buy, you have to carry with you. Moving additionally allows you to try a new neighborhood and find a home with more desirable features. But most importantly, moving is a great way to build net worth.

Making the housing two-step most rewarding requires finding the right house. The perfect target home sells for 20% below market value. This home may be difficult to spot, but the reward makes the effort worthwhile. Usually, the home needs cosmetic work and a little imagination to reach its full value.

For example, suppose you buy a "fixer-upper" for $80,000. Over the next two years, you bring it up to its full market value. At the same time, assume that housing prices increase at the conservative rate of 3% per year. After two years you have a home worth $106,000. If the costs of fixing up the home and selling it are 5% of its market value, you can pocket $20,700 tax-free at the end of two years. But instead of buying a sports car, you put the whole $100,700 ($106,000 sales price minus $5,300 costs) into a new home that is similarly priced 20% below market. If you keep repeating the procedure over the years, your net worth will grow like this:

Year	Initial Price	Initial Value	Value after 2 yrs	Cost of Repairs and Sale	Net	Tax Free Gain
2	$80,000	$100,000	$106,000	$5,300	$100,700	$20,700
4	$100,700	$125,875	$133,428	$6,671	$126,756	$26,056
6	$126,756	$158,445	$167,952	$8,398	$159,554	$32,798
8	$159,554	$199,443	$211,409	$10,570	$200,839	$41,285
10	$200,839	$251,049	$266,112	$13,306	$252,806	$51,967
12	$252,806	$316,008	$334,968	$16,748	$318,220	$65,414
14	$318,220	$397,774	$421,641	$21,082	$400,559	$82,339
16	$400,559	$500,699	$530,741	$26,537	$504,203	$103,645
18	$504,203	$630,254	$668,070	$33,403	$634,666	$130,463
20	$634,666	$793,333	$840,933	$42,047	$798,886	$164,220
Total						$718,886

With no other changes in lifestyle, the housing two-step lets you accumulate, tax-free, $718,886 in 20 years.

Supercharged Savings

Most everyone wants to get rich quick. High yield investments can provide a fast track to simplicity. For example, in the 1990's, technology stocks often returned 50–100% per year. However, more recently, those stocks have tumbled down, leading some to rethink their retirement plans. As a rule, the higher the rate of return, the higher the risk.

As described in the Epilogue, real estate served as a super-charged savings plan for me. When I started investing, using borrowed money, my effective rate of return was astronomical. For example, a $100,000 house, bought with $20,000 down, remodeled for $5,000 and sold for $120,000 two months later, yields an effective 480% annual rate of return. Now that I have retired and become a passive investor, real estate contracts provide a relatively safe 8% rate of return.

Real estate has been a road to wealth for many. It worked for me. But remember, the higher the rate of return, the higher the risk of loss. Your skills, interests, motivation and risk tolerance will determine the rate of return you earn on your investments.

The Best Path

The best path is your path. Your dream is unique. Your family and financial situation are unique and your path to simplicity will be unique. This book suggests values and strategies that may be helpful, but it is up to you to develop a plan to fit your situation. Take some time now to consider your net worth, income and expenses and sketch a path to simplicity.

CHAPTER 10

PURSUE YOUR DREAM

When the path to simplicity leads you to the clouds, you are free to pursue your dream. Exercise nine asked what is most important to you. Exercise four asked what you are too busy to do. Both answers represent a logical analysis of your situation. They may say little about your dream. Exercise five asked, "If I had unlimited time, money and talent, I would…." Exercise five strips away the logical excuses and exposes the dream.

This may challenge what you usually think and I invite you to explore that challenge. Rather than rejecting the dream as unreasonable, take a few days and search your mind. Perhaps that dream is what you really desire.

But in the end, this book is about you and only you will define your dream. And your dream is not static. After years of traveling you may decide to work with children. After trying writing, you may study music. I encourage you to acknowledge your dream, to use it as a carrot on the path to simplicity, and when you are free of paid work, to pursue it full time.

Exercise six asked, "If I lost my job today I would…." If your answer was one of panic, think about following some of the suggestions in this book. When you calmly answer with something like, "take a trip around the world," you will know you have made great progress.

Most people lead lives of quiet desperation. I'll be darned if I will. Hopefully you now feel the same. Good luck on your path to simplicity.

EPILOGUE: MY PATH

The previous chapters describe the changes in values that moved me along the path to simplicity. This Epilogue focuses on investments I made that freed me from paid work in eight years.

Live Fast, Die Young, Leave a Beautiful Corpse

I wish someone had provided me with the information in this book when I was young. Fresh out of college, I had a good paying job and put away $20,000. At that time in the 1970's, safe investments paid 15% and more. If I had known then what I know now, I could have invested the money and without adding another dime would have had $466,000 by the time I was 42.

But being a young man, I did not have that knowledge. I quit my job, traveled around the country and eventually ended up in graduate school. I did not think about money again until I was in my 30's.

When I was young, I never expected to become middle aged or old. I was too caught up in the excitement of life. Perhaps, as an earlier generation joked, I wanted to "live fast, die young and leave a beautiful corpse."

One day when I was 34, I found myself living in a dive apartment, driving a junk car and coping with $30,000 in student loans. I had a modest paying job working for state government, but even with thrifty living, the day I could pay off the student loans was years away.

Around this time I realized I probably would not die young. The more I thought about it, the more I realized I did not want to die old and poor. So I started reading about money. I checked a number of books out of the library. I decided to begin paying as much as possible on my student loans, while also saving to buy a house.

I used the trick of taking an amortization chart and adding the principal of future loan payments to my scheduled payment, therefore making double and triple principal payments on my loan. I would cross off the extra payments on the amortization chart and tell myself how many months of payments I saved. The same trick works on credit card and mortgage payments. For example, on a $100,000 mortgage at 6%, the regular monthly payment is $599.55. If you add $100.05 to the first payment, you will effectively pay for two months. Cross off the first two principal payments on your chart. On the second month add $101.05 to your regular payment and you will have effectively reduced the principal due by four payments, simply by sending in two regular payments and an extra $201.10.

Payment Number	Principal	Interest
1	$99.95	$500
2	$100.05	$499.50
3	$100.55	$499.00
4	$101.05	$498.50
5	$101.56	$497.99

Your lender can provide you with an amortization chart, or you can amortize your mortgage online at www.hughchou.org/calc/mort.html and your credit card payments online at www.bankrate.com/brm/calc/Minpayment.asp.

Building Skill and Capital

A year later, I had paid off more than $10,000 of student loans. My father died, leaving me $30,000. I paid off the remaining student loans and purchased an interest in a cooperative condominium. At the same time, I shifted the money I had used to pay down student loans to buying mutual funds. With the cooperative condominium, I accomplished an early goal, having a home that I was not embarrassed to have others see.

Six months later, I bought my first house. It was a simple two bedroom, one bath home on a main road. It cost $70,000. After the offer went through, I could not sleep. I imagined the $400 a month payment would bankrupt me. But it turned out to be a great investment.

After buying the home, I read a useful book, <u>Renovating Your Home for Maximum Profit,</u> by Dan Lieberman and Paul Hoffman. I knew nothing about improving houses and had no handyman skills. However, I made a few changes. I removed a 1950's wooden bookcase that served as a barrier between the dining area and living room. I replaced it with a half wall of glass blocks. I added some cabinets and counter space in the kitchen. I repainted the cabinets and put self-adhesive tiles on the floor. I remember putting a motion detector light by a side door. I must have read the installation instructions five times. I was so nervous that I would install it wrong and burn down the house. Little did I imagine that years later installing a house full of light fixtures would be a simple task completed in an afternoon.

I continued to save money and six months later found a better house. It had 3 bedrooms, 1.75 baths, a fireplace and was located off the main road in a nicer neighborhood. It was an ugly house. The roof shingles were peeling and the older owner had a menagerie of animals who made the carpet stink. The offer went through at $86,000.

I put my first house up for sale at $89,000 and took an offer of $87,650 on the first day. I had not invested more than $1,000 and 20 hours in the first house. After all expenses, I made $15,000. I made more in six months in my spare time than I could have saved working full time for a year and a half! That really got my attention. Additionally, at that time federal law did not tax home sale profit if you rolled it into another primary residence, which I did. With very little work in six months I made $15,000 tax-free. And at the same time, I was able to stay at my regular job and continue regular savings. Suddenly my financial picture looked very different. I had a net worth of $33,000 and I was moving forward.

The second house required more extensive renovation. I hired workers to install the roof, transform an odd formal living room into a home office with closets (so it also counted as a fourth bedroom) and to install new vinyl and carpet.

Within a year, I was ready to move on. I found a government repo house for $95,000. It was in a better neighborhood and had a two-car garage. Like the previous house, it needed a roof, paint and carpet. I sold house #2 on a one year lease/purchase agreement with a sales price of $115,000. The rent was $200 more than my payment, so I had a small cash flow plus $20,000 more net worth. And once again, I kept working at my regular job and adding to my regular savings.

After six months in house #3, I got itchy feet again. House #4 had not been modified since it was built in the early 70's. Each room had different colored shag carpet and brightly striped wall paper. But otherwise it was an attractive home in a good neighborhood. Once again, I hired out most of the work. A painter quoted a ridiculous $2,000 to paint the interior, so I painted it myself. I also had to figure out how to replace a broken toilet.

I sold house #3 on a lease/purchase agreement for $129,000. The buyer did not exercise his purchase option, so house #3 became a rental property, adding $150 per month to my cash flow.

About this time, my net worth was $100,000. Two rental properties provided a few hundred extra dollars income per month and I decided I would build up to ten rentals and quit my paid job.

I borrowed on the equity of house #4 and purchased my first investment only house—that is a house I did not live in, but held solely for investment purposes. I leased it without improvements for $750 per month, resulting in a positive cash flow of $200 per month. Within a few months I added another rental house.

Along the way, federal tax law changed so that you could take profit tax-free from any home you lived in as your primary residence for two years. I changed my strategy and began living in each primary residence for two years. After two years I would sell and take the profit tax-free. I rolled the profit into the next house, so I kept moving to larger and more impressive homes that needed just a little "TLC" to reach their full value.

I built up to six rental homes when I realized that, although profitable, rental houses bring tenant problems. There was an accidental shooting of a child in one of my rentals. Another tenant was chronically late paying. My net worth and income were increasing dramatically and I decided I no longer wanted rental properties.

I discovered that what I really enjoyed was making ugly homes more attractive. I bought ugly houses, fixed them and sold them on a refinance, or in special circumstances (for a difficult to sell house or when I desired a stream of income) on a real estate contract—where I acted as the bank and loaned the buyer money.

Buying on the Bell Curve

One of the most valuable things I learned in college is that all human behavior falls along a bell curve. For example, most people are average height, but a few are very tall and a few are very short. The same rule applies to intelligence. The same rule also applies to house pricing (Figure 5). Most house prices fall in the middle of the bell curve. A few are way overpriced, and a few are underpriced. The underpriced houses move quickly, but they are out there. My goal became to buy a house under-priced by 20% and to sell it slightly below market value so it moved quickly.

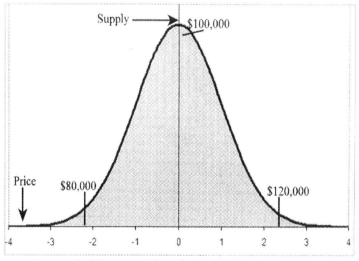

Figure 5. House pricing falls along the bell curve.

With each house I remodeled, I learned a new skill. I figured the people I paid to work, as nice as they were, were not brain surgeons. Each of their skills was learnable. From a start of painting walls, I learned to lay laminate floors. Later, I added ceramic tile. Along with the tile, I learned to replace toilets and to do some basic plumbing. On another house, I read books about electricity and learned to wire lights and outlets. I picked up some drywall skills and learned how to replace windows. Through a combination of reading, watching, asking questions and figuring things out myself, I learned many skills.

On each remodel, I worked fast. I would take one week vacation from work, sandwiched between two weekends, totaling nine days. Sometimes I was very lucky. My record time between buying a house and collecting the funds from the sale was 27 days. The longest was four months.

I sold each house without a realtor and therefore kept more of my earnings than some investors.

Five years after I bought my first house, I reduced paid work to 24 hours a week. I bicycled to work and walked to the gym. I significantly cut back on driving. I continued to use vacations to remodel homes.

Lessons Learned

Over the years, I have bought and remodeled 37 houses. Some of the lessons I learned as a real estate investor are:

1.   Buy ugly houses. You get paid for having vision.

2.   No risk, no reward. No one will throw money at you.

3. Do not buy a house that you would not (after it is fixed up) live in.

4. Buy a house with good "bones," that is, with cosmetic damage, but no real structural problems.

5. Do not buy a house on a main road (front, back or side).

6. Do not buy a house near a nuisance (bar, dairy, store, drive through window, etc.).

7. Do not buy a house with an odd floor plan.

8. Put a "feature" into each remodel; for example, a marble entry, glass blocks in the master bedroom, or wood floors in the living room.

9. Learn from model homes. Builders follow market trends and incorporate them into their models. Visit them to learn styles. But remember, put your remodel on par with the builder's more expensive model—it won't cost you much more but it will make your home more desirable.

10. Do it right. Do not hide flaws, fix them.

11. Buy 20% below market, sell slightly below market.

12. When rating vision, on a scale of 1–10, the average home buyer's vision is zero or one. Do not show a house until it is done.

13. When you sell a house, learn from hotels. Even though someone else stayed in your hotel room the previous night, when you arrive the odors are masked, the fixtures are clean and the room is bright. Your home for sale should be the same.

14. Treat everyone who visits your home for sale as a buyer and with respect.

15. There is only one thing wrong with that house—the price. All of these rules can be overridden if the price is right.

Living in the Clouds

Seven years after I bought my first house, I had built a nest egg in my spare time big enough to allow me to quit paid work. I wanted to quit, but I did not. I felt insecure about living on my investments and I wondered if I had enough.

Finally, eight years after I began investing, the petty demands and controlling attitude of my boss got to me. I quit. Rationally, I knew I had enough to survive, but still I was insecure. After quitting work, I kept investing in houses. In fact, my income after quitting was greater than when I was working.

Since quitting paid work, I have passed a few more milestones. Over the years, I moved to larger and larger homes. Finally, I found myself in a 3,300 square foot mini-mansion in an elite neighborhood. The home was an investment, but I never felt comfortable in it. It was not consistent with a simple life style. But I stayed two years so I could take the profit tax-free. When I sold the house, I paid off my last remaining mortgage and entered the "cash only" zone. My net worth is completely mine. I make payments to no one.

Since selling the big house, I have moved to a modest townhouse. I have remodeled it to my liking and installed zero maintenance landscaping. The utilities and taxes are a fraction of what I paid in the big house.

For me, investing in real estate provided a fast path to simplicity. As I write this, I am resigning from real estate investment and preparing to spend full time pursuing what interests me. Although real estate remains a hobby, my dream is to write and travel. This book is a first step.

I suppose if I kept working I could have had a mansion with a grand view and a garage with a Hummer, a Mercedes and a Corvette. But I know I am going to die. I know I have an uncertain number of days left to pursue my dreams. Rather than trading my time for more and fancier material goods, I choose to have all my time free to do what interests me.

At this point in my life, I live simply, exercise regularly and have little desire for material things. I remember when I was working how nice Sundays felt. Now every day for me is a

Sunday. Sometimes people wonder how I retired so young. This book is my explanation.

SHARE THIS BOOK

Did you enjoy <u>Rational Simplicity</u>? If so, don't put it on the bookshelf, pass it on to a friend. Just for fun, write your first name and hometown on this page and see how far your copy of <u>Rational Simplicity</u> can travel.

For additional copies of <u>Rational Simplicity</u>, contact you local book store or buy online at iuniverse.com.

0-595-34214-0

Printed in the United States
41129LVS00006B/268-276